BE INSPIRED TO SUCCEED

Ten Crown Jewels to Succeed

By Lawrence Alexander Jr.

Published by Alexander's Enterprise, LLC.

COPYRIGHT © 2017 Lawrence Alexander Jr.

ISBN: 978-0-578-19847-7

**Be Inspired to Succeed
Ten Crown Jewels to Success**

Written by: Lawrence Alexander Jr

FIRST EDITION/FIRST PRINTING

Printed in Collierville, TN USA

InstantPublisher.com, Inc.

lalexander10jr@gmail.com

I Dedicate this book to
Lawrence Alexander III
Lauren Brook Alexander
Jonathan Lawrence Alexander

Never give up on your dreams.

"The future belongs to those who prepare for it today."

Malcolm X

Table of Contents

BE CONSISTENT

BE DISCIPLINED

INTRODUCTION

Do not allow this world to place its conditions on you; you place your conditions on the world. You have no limits. Do not be limited by what you can see; be on fire with what you see yourself doing.

Your ability to accomplish greatness lies in what you are willing to do to get there.

"Success is a continuing thing. It is growth and development. It is achieving one thing and using that as a stepping stone to achieve something else."

John C. Maxwell

BE CONSISTENT

BE DISCIPLINED

1 – MAKE A COMMITMENT TO LEARN DAILY

When you make it your goal to grow by learning something new every day, it will empower you to reach your greatest goals in life. Take time daily to read, listen, or study something in your field, vision, dream, or whatever you feel God has placed on your heart to accomplish.

Remember: Attaining knowledge is the easy part; using wisdom to apply it is the hard part.

Take time out of each day, even if it is only five minutes, to learn and gain knowledge in your field and areas of interest. Strive towards your dreams. Grow and work your way up to devoting more time to this endeavor. With the technology we have today, smartphones and search engines allow you to look up information just about anywhere. There is no excuse not to read, study, and research any field you are interested in.

***

If what you are learning is not contributing to a change in how you act or think, then you are reading for enjoyment instead of personal growth. What generates results is actually physically doing and acting on what you learn and read consistently. This sounds obvious, and yet this is an area where people fail again and again.

***

If you read about personal growth, dreams, and visions, listen to audiobooks, go to workshops, and so on, but fail to apply what you already believe will make a difference for you, you will consistently go around in circles. At best, you will get some entertainment value from the material you are absorbing, but you will likely waste your time.

Remember: Find what works for you and apply it.

The whole point of absorbing new information on personal growth is for you to apply what you learn so that you can achieve better results than you are getting now. Better results may mean being able to achieve that dream of being your own boss, earning more money, being physically fit, or being more organized.

THERE IS A DIFFERENCE BETWEEN KNOWLEDGE AND WISDOM. KNOWLEDGE IS INFORMATION; WISDOM IS KNOWING HOW TO USE IT.

James 1:5 – If any of you lacks wisdom, you should ask God, who gives generously to all without finding fault, and it will be given to you.

BE CONSISTENT

BE DISCIPLINED

2 – BE WILLING TO STEP OUT IN FAITH

Faith is like gravity: it is a law if you believe all is possible. Just like gravity, what goes up must come down. What you have the faith to believe can, and will, come to pass.

Remember: All that a man achieves, and all that he fails to achieve, is the direct result of his own thoughts and faith.

There are two types of people: those who are full of confidence and faith, and those who are full of doubt and fear. Practice exercising your faith from the time you wake up in the morning until the time you lay down at night. Make a conscious effort to walk by faith in your everyday life. God has given every man the measure of faith he requires. Whatever you are believing God for, He has given you the faith for it.

Remember: Faith cannot exist with doubt and fear. When believing, you must believe with confidence.

YOU MUST CONQUER DOUBT AND FEAR. ONLY THEN WILL YOUR EVERY THOUGHT BE ALIGNED WITH POWER AND FAITH.

James 1:6 – But when you ask, you must believe and not doubt, because the one who doubts is like a wave of the sea, blown and tossed by the wind.

3 – MOTIVATE YOURSELF

You cannot get much done in life if you only work on the days when you feel good. The individuals who go far do so because they motivate themselves and give life their best, regardless of how they feel. To be successful, you must persevere.

Remember: Motivating yourself is ninety percent attitude. Once you decide to think thoughts of greatness, success, and achievement, you will never be defeated in your mind.

Make it a habit every day to encourage yourself. Look at yourself in the mirror and make positive affirmations that inspire and motivate you. You are what you do daily; so in everything you do, wherever you are – your walk, your talk – do everything in a positive manner.

***

Create an environment that inspires and motivates you by putting pictures, objects, and words all around you that keep you encouraged. These things will feed your imagination and push you to stay motivated to succeed.

Remember: Be more than a conqueror; be the head not the tail, be above only and not beneath.

Find those thoughts that inspire and motivate you, whatever they may be. It is time to discover your power through inspiring yourself.

"If you can't fly then run, if you can't run then walk, if you can't walk then crawl, but whatever you do you have to keep moving forward."

Martin Luther King Jr.

LEARNING HOW TO BE CONSISTENT IN MOTIVATING AND ENCOURAGING YOURSELF, WILL OPEN INFINITE DOORS OF SUCCESS IN YOUR LIFE.

1 Samuel 30:6 – And David was greatly distressed; for the people spoke of stoning him because the soul of all the people was grieved, every man for his sons and for his daughters: but David encouraged himself in the LORD his God.

BE CONSISTENT

BE DISCIPLINED

4 – CHOOSE YOUR THOUGHTS WISELY

Your thoughts are responsible for everything you experience in life. You are essentially a maker of yourself by the thoughts you wield, choose, and encourage.

Remember: You must become one with your thoughts and ideas. You will always gravitate towards that which you secretly cherish or love.

Whatever your present environment may be, it will rise, fall, or remain with your thoughts, your visions, and your ideas. Start to create an environment right now that builds on your every thought of success.

***

Most people think that because they earnestly wish for or pray for something they desire, it will come to pass. Your earnest prayers are only gratified and answered when they harmonize with God's thoughts and actions. Find that place where you can get into sync and in rhythm with your thoughts, and let the infinite wisdom that God has prepared for you flow through you.

Remember: Most people are anxious to improve their circumstances, but are unwilling to improve themselves.

They stay in the same place professionally, physically, and mentally.

Think of your thoughts as a master swordsman who knows how to instinctively wield that sword to take advantage of his opponent. Set aside time to practice putting your most dominant thoughts of what you want to achieve in the forefront of your mind, and let those thoughts shape your life as they work on your behalf to give you the advantage to achieve literally everything you can think.

"Everything is energy and that's all there is to it. Match the frequency of the reality you want and you cannot help but get that reality. It can be no other way. This is not philosophy. This is physics."

Albert Einstein

EVERYTHING THAT HAS EVER BEEN INVENTED OR MADE, EVERY PERSON WHO HAS ACHIEVED SUCCESS, IT ALL STARTED WITH A THOUGHT.

Proverbs 23:7 – For as he thinks within himself, so he is.

BE CONSISTENT

BE DISCIPLINED

5 – TAKE HOLD OF THE TREASURE HOUSE WITHIN

Your imagination is truly limitless; if you can imagine it, you can become or create it. Everything that you are, everything that you will be, lies within you.

Remember: Starving the potential that is within you will hinder your growth.

Focus on the gifts and talents you have within you on a daily basis. Start when you wake in the morning with prayer and meditation. Take time out while driving to work, walking, or while you are just sitting around, to focus on that thing you desire the most.

Remember: By taking time to read, listen to audiobooks, and mediate on the goals and dreams of what you want to be and become, you take hold of your dream. And once you have taken hold of it, cling to it. Never let it go.

YOU ARE AS GREAT AS YOUR DOMINATE THOUGHT.

Genesis 11:6 – And the LORD said, Behold, the people are one and they have all one language; and this they began to do: and now nothing will be estranged from them, which they have imagined to do.

"Your hands are tied in action, but your hands are not tied in imagination and everything springs forth from the imagination. Everything."

Esther Hicks

6 – CULTIVATE GRATITUDE

The more you recognize God as your source, and are grateful for what He has given you, the more you will receive from Him. You cannot exercise more power without gratitude, for it is gratitude that keeps you connected to the power to believe.

Remember: There is a law of gratitude, and if you observe this law, you will get the results you seek.

Throughout your day, fix your mind on thanking God for what He has done for you. It is necessary to cultivate a habit of being grateful for every good thing that comes to you. Any and everywhere, give thanks continuously.

***

Focus on the good things God has done in your life; the more you fix your mind on God when good things happen in your life, the more you will receive from God, and the more continuously you will see all your hopes and ambitions come to pass.

THERE IS A LAW OF GRATITUDE, AND THIS LAW ALONE CAN KEEP YOU LOOKING TOWARD YOUR DREAMS AND PREVENT YOU FROM FALLING INTO THE ERROR OF UNBELIEF.

Colossians 3:17 – And whatever you do, whether in word or deed, do it all in the name of the Lord Jesus, giving thanks to God the Father through Him.

7 – WRITE YOUR VISION AND MAKE IT PLAIN

Let your vision be your motivation to achieve what you see. Your vision is a seed that you must nurture and water daily until your dreams come to pass.

Remember: God will give you the provision to achieve the vision in your heart.

Decide right now what you really want, and let God guide you. Once you are in the place He desires, everything else will fall in place in your life. You do not need to know how it will come about; just have unwavering faith that it will. Live fearlessly for your vision so that you may never allow doubt and fear to quench it.

***

Write your vision down. Create a vision board so you can see your vision daily. Never let a day go by where your vision is not before you.

IN ANY VISION, YOU HAVE TO TAKE THE FIRST STEP. WRITE IT DOWN AND BELIEVE GOD. TAKE THAT WHICH IS INVISIBLE, AND MAKE IT TANGIBLE TO YOU.

Proverbs 29:18 – Where there is no vision, the people perish.

8 – TAKE THE INVISIBLE AND MAKE IT VISIBLE

Just because you cannot see something, does not mean it is not tangible. Your idea is the invisible of what you desire to see.

Remember: If you can conceive the invisible, you can do the impossible.

Dream grand dreams; as you dream, you will become. As often as you dream your dream, is the prophecy of what you will uncover. Your thoughts, your visions, your ideas, will become as small as your strongest desire and as great as your prevailing passion.

***

Everything that has ever been created started with a thought, a mental picture, the invisible not yet made tangible. Your vision is an image of something that can be through the law of faith. Let your mind be the dominate picture of what you see, and how you see, your life and your future. Let the invisible inspire pursuit and energize you as you see your dream come to reality.

THE MENTAL VISION OF WHAT YOU KEEP SEEING WILL AFFECT WHAT YOU DO AND WILL HELP YOU BRING IT TO PASS.

2 Corinthians 5:7 – For we walk by faith, not by sight.

9 – PUT ACTION BEHIND YOUR DREAMS

Your personal actions must supplement your thoughts. Until you put action, not talk, behind your dreams, they will stay as memories headed nowhere.

Remember: God has infinite ways to work your dream out. It is up to you to take the necessary action to receive, believe, and take hold of your dream until you see it tangible in your life.

When you are looking to God for your vision, He is looking to you to act on what you are believing so He can step in and bring that thing to pass. Everything you are to be is within you. Your dreams that you dream are where you start to put action behind them.

Remember: Your work, and actions, prove your faith.

You can pray all day long, but if you really want to get God's attention and see your dream come to pass, you must take the next step and demonstrate your faith. Let your actions prove your faith. If your vision is to be in business for yourself, you must have an idea of what type of business you want to begin, and then you start looking into business opportunities. You may not have the financial resources, but by you doing your part, God will do the rest.

"Act like you are blessed. Talk like you are blessed. Walk like you are blessed. Put actions behind your faith and one day you will see it become a reality."

Joel Osteen

YOUR FAITH PICTURE WILL
INSPIRE YOU TO PURSUE YOUR
DREAM. YOUR ACTIONS
BEHIND YOUR FAITH PICTURE
WILL ENERGIZE AND PUSH YOU
TO UNLOCK THE FLOW OF
FAITH IN YOUR LIFE. EVERY
ACTION YOU DO TOWARDS
YOUR DREAM WILL BE A
SUBCONSCIOUS ATTEMPT TO
MAKE YOUR DREAM COME
TRUE.

Hebrews 11:1-2 – Now faith is confidence in what we hope for and assurance about what we do not see. This is what the ancients were commended for.

BE CONSISTENT

BE DISCIPLINED

10 – RECOGNIZE THAT YOUR DESTINY IS IN YOUR HANDS

Your destiny is ordered by you; it is your destiny to walk in what you believe your destiny to be. Your destiny has no limits. The only limits are those that you place on it.

Remember: Your destiny will lead you where your reasonable mind cannot.

Your destiny requires you to be in rehearsal each and every day. That means you visualize it in your mind and see the "me" to which you want to be. Your destiny will cause things you want to be created in the environment around you. Everything you are to be is within you. Your dreams that you dream are where you start to put action behind your destiny.

Remember: You must invest time into making your dreams happen. It is an evolving resolution that will push you to that desired end.

That means every single day, you need to be doing something pertaining to your destiny. For example, reading books in your desired destiny. Or, if you plan on going into business, research companies and create a plan.

You have to stay focused on what is in your thoughts, and that focus will bring the within to the out, and that will create a chain reaction of events that will open up doors that you have not thought of.

***

The strength of your efforts is the measure of the results you want to see.

BE CONSISTENT

BE DISCIPLINED

YOUR DESTINY IS THE SOLE REPRESENTATION OF YOUR DESIRE TO BE WHATEVER YOU CHOOSE TO BE.

Proverbs 16:3 – Commit your works to the LORD, and your plans will be established

CONCLUSION

In our daily routines in life, we lose focus. We think about things that have happened in our past – mistakes, relationships, failures, and things we could have avoided, when our focus should be on our future aspirations, goals, dreams, desires, and accomplishments.

When those past thoughts start to creep up in your mind, stop yourself and change your focus. Meditate on one of these inspired crown jewels to succeed.

Remember: the vision that you glorify in your mind is in throne in your heart. This is where you build your life, and by this you will become.

www.ingramcontent.com/pod-product-compliance
Lightning Source LLC
Chambersburg PA
CBHW071448040426
42445CB00012BA/1485